Signals

DARON KENNETH

authorHOUSE

AuthorHouse™
1663 Liberty Drive
Bloomington, IN 47403
www.authorhouse.com
Phone: 833-262-8899

Published by AuthorHouse 11/09/2020

ISBN: 978-1-6655-0059-3 (sc)
ISBN: 978-1-6655-0058-6 (e)

Print information available on the last page.

This book is printed on acid-free paper.

Contents

A Day I the Backyard

It is a wonderful day outside. I walk down from
The living room to the back porch and open the
Door. As I do, Shadow quickly darts out and
Begins pacing up and down the back wall of
The screens. He sees the birds a squirrel and
A rabbit. He stares at them just wishing that
He could be outside and chase them around the
Backyard. I sit on one of the chairs out there.
I take in all that is going on outside. Every
Once in a while I see the big bunny go from
The hedge to the neighbor's yard into ours.
He is getting to finally be a little brave and he
Doesn't run off like he used to. I am trying to
Tame him by just standing in the yard as he
Eats the grass that is growing on the lawn. We
Stare back and forth at each other. I don't
Move as he comes a little closer. I hope that
Over Tyme I can get him to warm up to me.
We just stare back at one another and I want
Him to know that he can trust me. Little by
Little I feed him some lettuce, hoping I can
Get him to where he is comfortable with me.
I smile at my new friend and hope he will feel
Safe in the backyard.

A Great Tyme of Year

Winter is over
Spring is finally here,
It's the greatest
Tyme of the year.
Leaves are growing
On the trees.
You can hear them blow
In a warm gentle breeze.
The rain falls gently
Throughout the hours
As you listen to
The morning spring showers.
The rain will make
The grass to grow
And all of the flowers
All in a row.
You can see the birds
With a worm in their beaks,
As they bring them home
For their babies to eat.
Everywhere that you look
You see nature thrive,
It's a great Tyme of year
To just be alive.

A Month of Mondays

Some days feel like they go on forever
Some days feel like they never end,
Some days are hard to get through
Some days feel like you just can't win.
Those are the days that you wish would fly by
Those are never, ever the fun days,
Those days are the ones that just creep by on and on
Those days are like a month of Mondays.
Some days are just plain depressing
Some days are just plain blue,
Some days are hard to get by them
Some days you just don't know what to do.
Those days you wish would just hurry by
Those days you just feel the pain,
Those days you just don't like at all
Those days you just feel all scatterbrained.
Some days you wish that never were
Some days feel like a living hell,
Some days are just a nightmare
Some days are like you're under a spell.
Those days you need someone to talk to
Those days you need someone on the phone
Those days you just need to muddle through
Those days you wish you weren't all alone.

Let's go sit in the sun,
Come on and have some fun.
We can walk down to the park,
We can stay till it gets dark.
Everything is growing in green,
The flowers are the nicest I've seen.
The trees are full of birds,
They speak without any words.
They sing their SpringTyme song,
It would be fun to sing along.
Looking up the sky is blue,
With lots of puffy clouds too.
We can have a picnic there,
I brought some foods to share.
The wind is blowing through the trees.
If you sit, you can feel the breeze.
We can enjoy the warm sunshine,
It will make you feel so fine.
We can go for a nice long walk,
While we enjoy a nice long talk.
A great way to share with a friend,
I hope that this day never ends.

Sitting in his rocking chair, he watches as the world
Goes by. He looks outward and sees the seasons
Come and go. With the passing of the seasons he
Feels the distance between himself and the world
Go by. When he was younger he Loved being out-
Doors and being an active member of society. But
As the years have passed he grew ever more distant
From the world outside and closer to the proximity
Of his walls and windows. Nowadays he is the
Captive audience of his television set. He sits by
The telephone and waits for phone calls that never
Come. He recalls the days when he was a much
More active member in his community. He waits
For visits from his children on the holidays. He
Loves spending Tyme with his grandchildren, but
They have grown up and don't visit him as often
As they once did. He is just waiting for the days
When they come to spend some Tyme with him
And he can tell them stories of his life from when
He was much younger and much more active. It
Seems that those days rarely come around anymore.
So he just stares at the windows and walls and
Reminisces about the days that have all but left
Him alone.

Alone in the afternoon, I sit and think about how
Much I miss my husband Richard when he is not
Around. It feels like I am the only one here even
Though I have my cat Shadow as my friend and
Companion. Even though he's here I still feel
All alone and sad. I often try to call someone up
On the telephone to try to use up some of that
Alone Tyme that I have on my hands during the
Week. I enjoy spending my Tyme alone once in
A while, but most of the Tyme I wish I had some-
One here to chat with during my weekdays, when
I am all by myself. I feel most lonely when I have
The afternoons after a long morning by myself. I
Really appreciate the Tyme we have together when
He is here by my side. I can turn on the television
Or talk to the cat, but it is not the same as the same
As the companionship of a real person, not to mention
Someone who really interacts with you and doesn't
Just want cat treats. There's something about that
Human to human contact that makes one feel adored
And appreciated.

As I Gaze Into Your Eyes

When I gaze into your eyes
I see the Love that's deep in there.
When I stare into your smile,
I see a grin that shows you care.

When you hold me in your arms
I feel a Love that won't let go,
When you kiss the way you do
I feel the Love I've come to know.

When we go for a walk
You always place your hand in mine,
When we just sit and talk,
You let me know that all is fine.

When I say the things I do
You know I mean every word,
When I hear the things you say
I know it's true Love that I've heard.

As Spring Weather Comes Shining Through

The wind is whistling in the trees,
I can feel the warmth of a gentle breeze,
The sun is bright, the sky is blue,
As the Spring weather comes shining through.
Clouds are forming in the air,
As I sit and enjoy the weather so fair,
There are shadows forming on the ground,
As chipmunks move without a sound.
The hedge is growing, the grass is green,
It's the prettiest shade I've ever seen.
The air is moving as the birds fly by,
The sky is so beautiful, it makes me cry.
The water falls down from the fountain,
As the shadows form in the shape of a mountain.
The air is fresh, the air is warm,
I see the bugs begin to swarm.
And I relax as the cat does as well,
As Mother Nature comes through so swell.
And finally at the end of the day,
The skies become a shade of gray.
And soon the sky will begin to rain,
As it make the flowers to bloom again.
And finally at the end of the day, the sun is setting,
This is truly the nicest Spring day that we're getting.

Autumn Leaves

As colorful leaves fall to the ground
They lay there still without a sound
Until someone walks upon them there,
Their beautiful scent will fill the air.
Then children jump in great big piles
As they do it will make them smile.
While they do the leaves will crunch
And they will have some fun a bunch.
In colors crimson, orange and yellow,
Their beauty helps to make me mellow.
They make no sound falling from trees
They collect in piles as you can see.
The trees will be bare till Spring's return
As people collect them in piles they burn.
There's nothing like the aroma of fall
When people let loose and have a ball.

Becky

Becky is the queen of the kitchen. She can make
Anything under the sun, (Not to mention that it
All tastes good!). Not only is she a talented cook,
She is also a great hostess. She is also a great
Party planner as well. Becky is kind to everyone
And I think we all will agree, she is one great
Sister-in-law as well. You would be so lucky to
Have her as a member of your family as I do too.
Not only is she handy around the kitchen, she is
Also a great friend. Not only is she beautiful on
The outside, but she is beautiful on the inside as
Well where it matters the most. She has got taste
And she has style, as well as the nicest smile you
Will ever come across now or later. Another thing
About Becky is that she is also a great mother to
All of her kids. You would be very lucky to have
Her as a member of your family. She's got taste,
She knows her way around a kitchen and she's a
Great mom as well. Try topping that!

Black

When you're not here
Colors fade to black
It's all different shades
In the hues that I lack.
The sun can be shining
Yet my life feels cloudy
I wish you were near
As I cry so loudly.
When I'm all alone
Nothing seems real
I wish you were here
I feel without zeal.
So please come back soon
I say it with passion
All has turned to gray
And it's gone out of fashion.

It's cold outside…the air is crisp and chilly,
The snow is frosty and deep, and where I look
I see bunny tracks giving me proof that there is
Still life out there, even if I don't see it around me.
I put out some old bread for the birds and some
Carrots for the rabbits in the yard. Its when the
Weather is at its worst that I think most about the
Wildlife in the neighborhood. At a frigid 7 degrees
It is so cold that your face hurts from the air. It
Burns your skin and frostbite is possible not long
After exposure to the freezing air.
The sky is a brilliant blue…it is beautiful yet it is
Deceiving. The sun's reflection is reminiscent of
A nice day in the Spring or Summer, but don't be
Fooled it is surely a cold wintry day. The hedge
In the backyard is alive with dozens of birds that
Are flying in and out of it. They are normally busy
Singing their songs of good cheer…not today.
They are staying in the hedge, just trying to stay
Warm. My cat, Shadow, normally sleeps in his
Bed on the couch, but not today. He is in the
Window trying to catch the sun's reflection and
Warmth as much as can be expected on a cold
Winter's day like today.

By the Beach

Growing up I remember
Days spent by the beach
Nothing seemed like
It was far out of reach.
But Tyme passed on by
The minutes turned to years
And now I'm alone
And you aren't here.
I wish I could turn back
The broad hands of Tyme
And bring back the days
When life seemed sublime.
Tyme has now been
Long since replaced
By the lines and wrinkles
Here all over my face.
So please come back soon
I feel all depressed
My youth has been taken
And all been repressed.

By Your Side

When I'm with you the sun always shines
A kiss from you is so divine,
I Love it when you hold my hand
A hug from you makes me feel grand,
I long to see the smile that's on your face
Spending Tyme with you makes my heart race,
I Love you because you're so sweet
The Love you give is such a treat,
When you're around I'm never alone
Your heart is the place I call home,
In all my life you are the best
Your Love is better than all the rest,
You're the reason I stand tall
With you by my side I'll never fall,
I'm so glad that you're my friend
You've helped my broken heart to mend,
You lift me up when I am weak
You make me strong when I feel meek,
When I am down you make me strong
It's by your side that I belong.

Cabin Fever

Take a look outside
To see the snow a half foot high
Just when you think this weather will never end
You'll see the sun will come shining through
Way up in the sky so blue
And bring this winter's season to an end
It will help your heart to mend
Oh, when the winters seem too long
When it seems all the good weather is gone,
Soon you'll come to think
That spring weather is on the brink
You'll feel that warm sunshine on your face
As you wish you were in a warmer place
Yes, the winters seem so wrong
And the bad weather is here too long
So take a look outside
To see the snow so high
And just when you think that the winter will never end
The sun will come shining through
Way up in the sky so blue
The sun will bring the bitter season to an end.

Carol Ann

We've been friends fo thirty plus years
We've shared some laughter and some tears,
She makes me smile when I feel low
She always has her own special glow,
I Love her because she's so kind
A truer friend I'll never find,
She always knows the right thing to say
She can always brighten a darkened day,
We like to get together and go out to eat
Spending Tyme with her is such a treat,
She has a green thumb that helps plants grow
She's one of the nicest people I know,
We enjoy Tyme together, we always have fun
I know we'll be friends till my days are done,
She knows how to bake, she knows how to cook
She can make you smile with just one look,
She has a great demeanor, it shows in her smile
She never gives in, she goes the last mile,
We can spend Tyme together just listening to tunes
I know we'll be getting together real soon,
I know we'll be friends for all of Tyme
I'm so very glad she's a friend of mine.

Corina

Corina is my other sister-in-law. She is always the
Life of the party! She can take a boring get together
And make it all worth while. Corina is beautiful on
Both the inside as well as the outside, not to mention
A beautiful soul as well. She has one of the kindest
Hearts that you will ever meet. Corina is the kind
Of person you pray she ends up playing on your
Team. She will stick up for the underdog and she
Will leave you laughing your butt off. Corina is
Always busy working on some project or other
And she can always fit ninety hours into just only
Twenty-four, (and how she manages to do it is her
Little secret). Corina has a style that is always in the
Forefront of her life. She knows which clothes are
Cool and always has the best haircut of the bunch
Of us. She always knows just what to say to make
A bad day better. You couldn't find a truer friend
That is more Loving than she is to her kids, and
Her husband. You go girl!

Creep

You helped me to lose my soul,
While Loving you was my goal.
You went and wasted all my Tyme,
You're not even worth a dime.
You went and helped to break my heart,
You went and blew my mind apart.
You made fun of what I said,
You made me wish that I was dead.
You went and made me feel insane,
You went and blew apart my brain.
You went and used me till the end
My heart and mind will never, ever mend.
You were never really nice,
Your heart was always cold as ice.
You took whatever you could take,
Then you caused my heart to ache.
Your soul was always as cold as steel,
You don't even care how much I feel.
You were never really kind,
Then you went and trashed my mind.
You went and acted so, so tough
I have finally had enough.

Crying

For everyone in this world, there is a Tyme that they
Experience sadness. Often when we are sad we come
To a point where the sadness is overwhelming and we
Cannot take the emotional ride. It can cause and finally
Come to where the sadness makes us lose control of
Our emotions and we begin to cry. Crying is like a
Cleansing of our emotional selves. Some people when
They are sad cannot handle the overwhelming feelings
And let the process of crying to begin. When we cry
We let the feelings we are having out and let the process
Of healing begin to work it's way through us. Some
People refuse to cry because they see it as a weakness.
However, crying is the beginning building block of our
Emotional selves. Holding in all of the feelings we
Have inside tears at the tapestry of our emotional system.
Everyone finds something that they need to let loose of
Emotionally and start to rebuild their feelings at a great
Loss. Most importantly we need to begin to heal our-
Selves and crying lets that process to begin.

Dana is my friend, Dana is my sister,
When she is not around I miss her.
We like talking on the phone,
She keeps me company when I'm alone.
She brings me up when I feel sad,
When I'm angry, she makes me feel glad.
Dana has long and dark brown hair,
When we get together, we make a good pair.
She is thoughtful she is kind,
SomeTymes she can read my mind.
She is small, she doesn't take up much space,
She also has a beautiful face.
She likes to meditate every day,
She remembers all of the things that I say.
Dana takes good care of her cats,
She is always thin and never fat.
Dana was the favorite child of my father,
I'm so glad to be her big brother.
If I'm the sun, then she is the moon,
I hope we get together real soon.
We like to go places together
Spending Tyme with her is always a pleasure.

Days in the Grays

The skies are gray again today for the second week
In a row. There's no sunshine to trickle down and
Light up the ground all around us. There's something
About having a lot of sunny weather to cheer up one's
Self. The gray skies are lifeless and cold leaving you
To feel alone. When the sun is out and shining, you
Get a feeling of warmth that you don't get when your
Days are all in the grays. I so enjoy getting out on the
Porch and enjoying the light from the sun. Even when
It is extremely hot you get that feeling like a friend is
Guiding you along on your day. You can almost hear
The life breathing into the surroundings when the sun
Is shining her Love down here on the Earth. The other
Nice thing about the sun is that she gives us the nice bit
Of color we call a suntan when she's shining her rays
Down here on us. The entire Earth seems so much more
Alive when the sun is sharing her warmth with us on a
Nice sunny day. Here's to the sun…may she forever
Light our way down here on planet Earth.

Dear God

Dear God, I'm praying to you with every breath I take
And every movement and with every step that I make.
I once feared dying but not now at all anymore
I relish stepping through that final heaven's door.
Where I will meet up again with the friends I've lost
And to then see my father again at what a great cost.
I will leave this wonderful world left behind
To get to another state of soul and of mind.
For God has in mind the perfect little plan
For all of his creatures and each living man.
I know God hears me, I'm ready to come home
To my final place in heaven, where I long to go.

Depression

Depression sets in
Despite the good weather
I long to feel
How I do when we're together
I miss your kisses
I miss them so much
I'm longing to feel
Your warm Loving touch
The places I go
Don't feel right
When I'm all alone
Day turns into night
Everywhere I turn
Are things that remind me
Of how our Love was
When you were here beside me
I miss the Tymes
We had so much fun
So please come back soon
And make all my sadness done.

She was like my second mother
Oh, how much I really Loved her.
She taught me to be kind,
And she helped me to be refined.
She had such a gentle touch,
I cared for her oh, so much.
We always had so much fun,
She treated me just like her son.
She had dark and auburn hair,
And her skin was oh, so fair.
How she Loved my sister and I,
She taught me to always try.
I was sad and young when she died,
Now she is my angel guide.
I wish I could tell her,
How much she meant to me.
I know she's in heaven,
And her soul is free.
She always took us out to eat,
She taught us to be clean and neat.
Her eyes were dark and black as coal,
She was such a beautiful soul.

Down and Blue

I'm feeling down and feeling blue
There's not much more that I can do,
There's not much more that I can say
To fight the way I feel today.
I wish I didn't feel so low
I don't know how much lower I can go.
I feel so down and feel so sad,
I'm tired of feeling down and bad.
I hope that one day I'll feel good
And feel more like the way I should.
I feel so down and feel so crappy,
I dream of the day I'll be feeling happy.
If life is a color then mine is black,
It's the joy in life that I truly lack.
I'm living a life that has no sun,
I'm tired of being used by everyone.
I guess that it's best that I live alone
I'll stay this way till my life is done.

Down By the Pool

The sun is warm
Down by the pool,
It's the perfect way
To stay nice and cool.
We can splash around
And have some fun,
As we soak up the rays
Just enjoying the sun.
We can bring along
The camera too,
So I can take some
Great pictures of you.
When it gets cool
We'll enjoy the breeze,
As the wind blows slowly
Through all of the trees.
We should bring
The radio along,
So we can listen
To our favorite songs.
We can't forget
Something to eat,
And something to drink,
It will be such a treat.
At the end of the day
We'll make our way home,
A much better way
Than spending it alone.

Down in the Blues

I'm feeling down and sad today,
I haven't got that much to say,
I wish I didn't feel so bad
I'm oh, so tired of feeling sad,
One day up, the next day down
One day a smile, the next a frown,
My emotions have me feeling so low
I don't know how much lower they can go,
Some days I spend the whole day crying
And some days I even feel like dying,
Some Tymes it helps to be with friends
On days I feel I've reached the end,
It's hard to live when you're not feeling well
It's like I'm living a life in hell,
So I spend Tyme with my husband Rich
He's good at helping me find my niche
SomeTymes I spend Tyme with Shadow, my cat
He helps lift my moods wherever I'm at,
I'm tired of living a life so blue
Though there's not much more that I can do,
So I take some Tyme to take my meds
And spend a lot of Tyme in bed,
Perhaps one day I'll be feeling good
As I try so hard to fix my mood,
Oh, my moods are changing like the weather
I hope one day I'll be feeling better.

Dreaming of Tomorrow

I'm just dreaming of tomorrow
Where my days are free of sorrow,
Where my days are filled with bliss
They all start with just a kiss,
Where you are holding onto me
And it's all your Love that I see.
Then you put your hand in mine
Then I'll feel your Love divine,
You know that you are my perfect Lover
You turn me on like no other.
I'm so glad we're more than friends
I will be with you till the end.
So now I look deep in your eyes
That are often hidden in disguise
But now they're a warm shade of brown
They cheer me up when I feel down,
I'm so glad you've come to stay
May you never go away.

Dressed Up Tyme

As I stared at the photograph of my father, my
Grandmother and Great Grandmother, I was
Taken back in Tyme and place to many years
Gone by. I was amazed at how dressed up
Everyone was. The adults were all in their
Sunday clothes as they stood in front of the
Church doorway that I knew so well from my
Years growing up in Portage, Wisconsin. It
Was so refreshing to see people dressed up
And looking so dapper. That was a Tyme
When people got dressed up for Sunday mass.
It was a point in Tyme where church was the
Big event of the week and you would wear
Your best clothes for the day. How sad
That today church has become so relaxed and
It doesn't mean as much as it once did. My
Grandmother and Great Grandmother were
All dressed up so as to look their very best.
Today it doesn't seem to matter what you are
Wearing. Back in those days everything was
For show... the clothes, the cars, even the way
You styled your hair was for looking the part.
What a shame that people don't care about
Their appearances like they used to. I guess
That today people are lucky if they even make
It to church at all, let alone what they look like.
The days of looking dapper are gone.

Feel So Blue

I wish I was feeling happy,
I'm so tired of feeling crappy.
I wish I didn't feel so blue,
I'm just not sure what to do.
I feel so down and feel so sad,
I'm sick and tired of feeling bad.
I wish I had more real friends,
I want them around until the end.
I wish I didn't feel so low,
I'm not sure how much further down I can go.
I wish I felt better about my life,
I'm left here feeling full of strife.
I wish I didn't feel so old,
It feels like life has left me out in the cold.
I guess that's just the way life goes,
I'm feeling like life really blows.
I feel like I'm out of my tree,
I'm feeling like that's the way it's going to be,
If life is a season, then I'm the Fall,
I'm feeling like I'm oh, so small.
I pray one day soon I'll be feeling good,
I'm hoping I'll be feeling like I should.
I know my moods change just like the weather,
I'm trying so hard to keep it together.

Outside the sun is shining
The sky is a beautiful shade of blue,
You can see it all around,
As Mother Nature comes shining through.
I enjoy the smell of SpringTyme
The aromas are everywhere,
Spring has finally sprung
You can smell it in the air.
The lawn is gently growing,
As the grass grows all around,
It soon will need to be clipped,
Different shades of green abound.
The birds are making their nests
In the hedge and in the trees,
They are flying all around,
They enjoy the means to fly free.
I'm staring up to heaven,
I'm looking at the sky
I'm envious of all of the birds,
I wish that I could fly.
If I only had one wish,
I wish Spring would always stay,
So that everyday was perfect,
It would always feel this way.

Fill You With Bliss

I see you there sleeping,
As the night hours come creeping.
I would like to snuggle with you,
There's nothing that I'd rather do.
So come and give me a kiss,
It fills my heart with bliss.
And when you kiss me that way,
I know that you want to stay.
We can make it, us together,
We can make it last forever.
So come and kiss me now,
We can make it through somehow.
So while you're still sleeping,
And as the night hours come creeping,
I'd like to make Love with you,
The way that true Lovers do.
You know the way you kiss me that way,
You know it will make you want to stay.
Oh, please come and kiss me now,
We can make it last somehow.

The sun is shining bright today
And spring is everywhere.
The Earth is teeming with life
You can feel it in the air.
The grass is finally growing,
Its color is vivid and green,
It is growing all around
It is the nicest color I've seen.
The sky is full of birds
You can see them all around,
The ground is full of squirrels,
They move without a sound.
Spring is full of aromas,
You can take in all of the smells,
Different scents are everywhere,
Spring never smelled so swell.
I'm taking in the sunshine,
I can feel it on my face,
It feels so good to be alive,
The world is such a beautiful place.
The air is fresh and warm
The temperature is just so fine,
It feels so good to be outdoors,
The day is finally mine.
I'm listening to Mother Nature
And all of the sounds she makes,
Her noises are all around,
Spring is finally, now awake.

Find a Hand to Hold

When you're feeling low,
Feeling there's not far left to go
Till you get to the point
Where there's no turning back,
You need a hand to hang on
Before you're too far gone.
Then say a prayer or two
And take a leap of faith that's true
One to save you from the cold
And just remember you've got
So much for you to lose.
So when you're feeling low
And there's not far left to go
Till you get to the point
Where there's no turning back
Just find a friend to hang on
Before you're too far gone
And you've taken that last step
From here to the very end
Just say a little prayer or two
And take a leap of faith that's true.
Just find friend to hold
One to save you from the cold
Just remember you've got
So much for you to lose.

Across Tyme, across space
I see your face as you smile down on me.
Your eyes, they shine and reflect into my eyes.
It's so nice to see you again.
We speak beyond words
We communicate our thoughts with our eyes.
I smile at you and then you return the look to me.
There's so much you can say with just your grin.
It's so nice to just be with you today.
I gaze at your wings
You wear them so well.
Though I don't have mine yet
I will earn them in Tyme,
Someday I will no longer be here earthbound
On to heaven we both will fly side by side
We shall fly on into the light
Into Tyme we both shall descend,
Oh, to be with you forever more.

Outside the world is calling but inside my world
Has fallen apart. I gaze at the happenings just
Outside my door. I remember the days gone by
When I was so much younger. I looked forward
Each day to play with my friends. We spent all
Of our free hours just laughing and Loving the
Tyme that was ours. But like all of the others,
I have grown up and older with the passing of
Each day that goes by. My friends all have their
Own families and we rarely see each other any-
More. Like the passing of the days, life seems
To have all but passed me by. I miss the days
Of our younger years when we would spend
Hours and hours playing kickball, softball or
Swimming at the local lake or pool. Even
Playing games or swinging on a swing set held
Such an amazing amount of fun for us. The
Best part about being young was that the hours
Just seemed to crawl by leaving us Tyme for
Being youthful and just being kids. Now as I
Have grown older, the years pass by so quickly
That you can barely keep up with the passing
Hours on a clock. Oh, to be young and free
Again. I surely miss those days gone by.

Good God!

He rules over the darkness, He is the light,
He always makes what's wrong seem right.
He will comfort you when you are full of strife,
He's the master of souls, he is the giver of life.
He reminds us that we should always be kind,
He's the best friend you'll ever find.
He's always right, he's always fair,
He will always Love you and always care.
He made the universe, and he made the Earth,
He will forever fill your life with mirth.
He rules over the Guf, he is the king,
He will make your heart to sing.
He rules over heaven, he rules over the sky
He is always truthful, he will never lie.
He is pure thought, he is forever wise,
He will make your soul to rise.
He is always strong, he is never weak,
He will fill you with strength when you are meek.
He is always right, he is never wrong
He will fill your heart with song.
He will make your soul to raise,
He hears your thoughts when you sing his praise.
He will forever be your friend,
He will always be with you until the end.

Good To Be Me

Sitting on the back porch
I listen to the birds outside
The sun is finally shining
I can feel it in my eyes.
Resting on my lounger
Just taking in all the sounds,
The air feels warm and fresh,
There's warm weather all around.
Listening to Mother Nature
Just soaking up the SpringTyme
Noticing the light and shadows,
The day is finally mine.
Looking at the blue sky
Seeing clouds up everywhere
Looking at the wonderful shapes
Spring is finally in the air.
Feeling the sun on my shoulders
Soaking up the sunshine's rays
Everything is beautiful,
Today is the nicest of days.
Snuggling with my kitty
Watching him look all around
Noticing his ears to perk up
The Spring weather all abounds.
Laying in the sunshine
I feel so fine and free,
It's the perfect day outside,
It is finally good to be me.

Great Big Wild World

It's a great big wild world
We have here at our fingertips
The world is quite literally a push
Button away. Anything and everything
Ones imagination can dream up is now at
Our beckoned call. Outer space has been
Literally replaced by the inner space of the
Internet. Our big, huge universe has now
Fallen into the space of a return key.
Strangely interesting is this space
Has now been replaced by a
Keypad just a push
Button away.

Heaven's Show

With every step I take
I get closer to my end
I long to stay healthy
And myself to mend.
But life seems so much shorter now,
I hope to make it through somehow.
With my husband and my cat now by my side
It seems life is just one long, bumpy ride.
And I try to stand real tall
While avoiding every fall.
When my final number is called at last
I will look forward and I won't be aghast.
I shall be glad life is over and onto heaven I'll go
This crazy life is over, now on with heaven's show.

Here Tonight

Tyme lingers on
While I'm here by my flowers
Minutes seem to pass
That go on for hours.
Tyme stands still
And light disappears
All I feel is dark
When you aren't here.
Please come back soon
And make things alright
I'm hoping that you
Are back here tonight.
No matter what I do
All the days drag on by
I hope that you
Are soon here by my side.

I grew up in the small town of Portage, Wisconsin.
During the seventies and early eighties, I lived on
Howard Street for most of that Tyme. Looking
Back, I was lucky enough to live across from Lincoln
Park and I was able to spend most of my childhood
Growing up playing there. At the Tyme I lived there
I didn't realize how fortunate I was to be so close to
A park where my sister, myself and our friends could
Play and run around and play so freely as we did. It
Is sad that today, children don't have the option to
Enjoy the great freedom of the outdoors as we did.
I remember that during the summer vacation from
School, we felt free to have all the fun that we could
Find. Another great thing we had were the Parks and
Recreation folks who came to the park and instructed
Us in how to make crafts and play with the equipment
They brought to the park. Even if you didn't have any
To play with, the Parks and Recreation people brought
Them for the children to play with for free. My favorite
Craft that the instructed us in was how to make Plaster
Of Paris. We would pour it into the molds on one day
And paint them the next. Looking back now, I appreciate
Just how blessed we were to have a park to play at in
Our great big back yard.

I'd Spend Every Moment With You

The sky is blue and sunny,
The weather outside is warm
The air is fragrant and fresh,
The birds are flying in swarms.
My cat is laying in the shade,
He is staring all around,
He loves to hear the birds,
He Loves to hear their sounds.
The trees are getting leaves now,
They grow so nice and slow,
The birds like them for nesting,
In the wind they softly blow.
The wind is gently blowing
As I sit here in the sun,
Mother Nature is controlling the weather,
It's the perfect day to have fun.
The lawn is slowly growing,
It is full and teeming with life,
Little life forms are moving all over it,
This day is free of strife.
I wish every day was a sunny day
That the skies were always so blue,
I would celebrate every moment I had,
I would spend every moment with you.

If I Can't Sleep…

It's 2:00 a.m. and I can't sleep…so I lay here
Watching you sleeping. I know that you are
Dreaming, and I hope that you are dreaming
Of me. I lay still and watch you breathing as
You inhale and exhale laying there. You are
At peace with the world and it shows. I can't
Help but stare at your handsome face and realize
Just how lucky I am to have you in my life.
Not only are you handsome, you are wise and
Very kind as well. I can't help but feel so very
Privileged to be the person that you are married
To. You indulge me in the things that you buy
For me. Not only is it a nice thing to do, but
It is a very kind thing to do as well. I so very
Much appreciate all the things that you do for
Me. I Love you so very, very much. Seeing
You so relaxed and serene, makes me relax
And cam down. Hopefully it is long enough
For me to finally fall back to sleep. Either way
I win…if I fall back to sleep I win, and if I don't
I can just enjoy watching you sleeping and
Dreaming. Hurray for me!

If I Was With You

I'm all alone
As I sit here and cry
I'll feel down and blue
Until the day I die.

I feel so awful
There's a storm in my head
Just feeling this way
Makes me wish I was dead.

I feel so rotten
I don't know what to do
I know I'd feel better
If I was with you.

My head's a mess
And I feel so tired
But someday soon
I'll be manic and wired.

Until that day
Until I feel good
I'll keep taking
My meds like I should.

I'll Go For Another Walk

As I look into the sky,
I watch the clouds as they float on by.
I see dew upon the lawn
As the sun rises at dawn
The air smells so fresh and so good
As I peruse the neighborhood.
I see birds up in the trees,
While I feel I gentle breeze.
I go for a nice long walk
Around several city blocks.
I see a man go for a jog
As another walks his dog.
I can feel the sun shining bright
As I walk around in its light.
The weather is nice, the weather is cool
As I go for a walk around the school.
There are some geese in the park
As the clouds begin to grow dark.
I know that soon it will rain,
So I start to walk home again.
And soon as the rain begins to fall
I go inside to get away from it all.
And when the rain finally comes to an end
I'll go for another walk around the bend.

In Dreams...

I'm dreaming of summer and all that it holds,
I'm dreaming of Summer, I'm sick of the cold,
I'm dreaming of fishing somewhere on a pier,
I'm dreaming of the season that's so far from here...
I'm dreaming of taking a walk in the sand,
I'm dreaming of walking on warm, grassy land.
I'm dreaming of walking down to the park,
I'm dreaming of going for a stroll alone in the dark.
I'm dreaming of swimming all day at the beach,
I'm dreaming of a season that's now out of reach.
I'm dreaming of throwing and catching a ball,
I'm dreaming of the seasons Spring, Summer and Fall.
I'm dreaming of sitting outside while I eat,
I'm dreaming of walking around in bare feet.
I'm dreaming of going to Summerfest for some tunes,
I'm dreaming of gardening in the warm month of June.
I'm dreaming of going out of doors for some camping,
I'm dreaming of sitting on a lawn chair and napping.
I'm dreaming of laying and tanning in the sun,
I'm dreaming of water skiing just for fun.
I'm dreaming of enjoying a warm summer day,
I'm dreaming of just going outside to play!

Shadow loves to sleep in his fuzzy bed. He
Sleeps the greater part of the day away. When
He wakes he gives himself a bath. This can be
Anywhere from three to even five Tymes a day.
He is the cleanest cat that I know. He always
Smells good, unlike some cats that I've had in
The past. He's always very jovial and has a
Great demeanor. He likes to snuggle with me
In my bed when I go to sleep at night. That
Cat just Loves to take naps on and off during
The day. He snores when he sleeps during the
Afternoon and night. He can sleep through
Anything: the T.V., the radio and the stereo.
Shadow isn't a high maintenance cat like some
Of the cats that I have had in the past. He will
Always use his litter box, unlike some of my
Former other cats. Shadow is really a loud
Purring cat. He purrs like an engine that does
Not quit. He Loves to go outside on the porch.
He just Loves seeing the wildlife in the yard.
He just started to take a nap…I think I'll join
Him for a nap myself.

In My Room

If I'm sad and full of gloom
I just journey to my room,
It's the place I go to be alone,
It's the place that I call home.
It's the place where I sleep at night
It's the place I go to feel alright
It's the place I go to sleep in my bed,
It's the place I go to rest my head.
It's the place I go when I make Love,
It's the place I go to pray to God above.
It's the place I go to feel renewed,
It's the place I go when I've come unglued.
It's the place I go to have my dreams,
It's the place I go to hatch my schemes.
It's the place I go to snuggle with my cat,
It's the place I go to hang my hat.
It's the place I go to keep my clothes,
It's the place I go that nobody knows.
It's the place I go with art on my walls,
It's the place I go when I'm feeling small.
It's the place I go where my flag's unfurled
It's the place I go to escape from the world,
It's the place I go when I feel trapped,
It's the place I go to take my naps.

In the Fresh Air

Hello there my friend
Let's go for a walk
As we both enjoy
Our Tyme as we talk.

We will reminisce
Our days we were young
And the Tymes we had
Just soaking up sun.

We remember our days
We spent at the park
Just playing our games
From dawn until dark.

At the nearby pond
We'd walk on the bogs
Where we caught some toads
And also some frogs.

At night we so liked
Just wishing on stars
While we caught lightning bugs
And put them in jars.

We spent every day
Without any cares
Just enjoying our Tyme
Out in the fresh air.

In the Moonlight

When the moonlight shines down upon the land,
It gives off the feeling of a softly flowing glow.
It is a glow that enlightens the whole world down
Here on Earth. The orb of light it gives warms
The world so we don't feel so alone in the dark.
Although the stars lighten the night as well, in
The big city you never get to see them because
Of the light from all the world around us. Some
People say that you can see the Man in the Moon
If you look closely up above, but you can't see
Him because of the other lights the city casts
Upon the land. The moon's glow is warm and
Enlightening so you can walk along and not feel
So alone. When you're by yourself and when
You go for a stroll in the evening, you feel like
A friend is walking beside you, keeping you
Company on your journey. When the moon
Is full, you can't help but feel like the hand of
God is shining down from the heavens above
Keeping your path well lit and as a friend he
Is also watching your every move to keep you
Safe from the harm that is the world of darkness
Without him.

In Winter

Winter winds come and winter winds blow,
Winter covers the ground in snow,
When the cold wind blows the snow around,
It stays cold without much sound.
It blankets the world in the color white,
It stays cold from dawn till night.
You can build a snowman out of doors
You can have snowball fights galore.
You have to shovel the sidewalks clean
You leave snow tracks where you've been.
You can see snow up in the trees,
You can see the snow upon the leaves.
When it gets cold roads turn to ice,
When you skate on ice it's really nice.
When it gets cold you can go inside,
Then later you take a sled and go for a ride.

It's Christmas Eve

It's Christmas Eve
And we're all asleep in bed,
Santa's with his reindeer,
They're pulling his sled.
And as we're sleeping
We dream of the gifts that we'll get,
Santa knows whether we're naughty or nice,
On that you can bet.
As for all of his reindeer,
Rudolf leads the pack,
They fly high in a wintry sky
Around the world, then they come back.
Then it's back to his workshop
Where all the elves make his toys,
The ones that warm the hearts of the good girls and boys.
And when he's done delivering
His toys all over the world
They're sure to warm the hearts
Of each and every good boy and girl.

Jump

You read about it all of the Tyme,
It makes you feel so sublime,
To live without it would be a crime.

If you say jump…
I ask how high…
If you say you can't…
I just say try…
If you say you could…
I just ask why…
If you say you would…
I just say fly…

And all the things you ever wanted
Will come true for you,
When you give up your old Tyme ways
It's Tyme to take a step into the electronic age.

If you say leap…
I ask how high…
If you say you can't…
I just say try…
If you say you could…
I just ask why…
If you say you should…
I just say fly…

Just a Bug

All alone I sit here
In a great big yard
Trying to contemplate
What it must be like
To be something as small
And little as an tiny insect,
Just trying to make it by,
Day by day in an area so
Small as the garden it lives in.
As human beings, we have the
Honor and beauty of being able
To traverse a space as renowned
As the earth for years and years.
In that moment and place we can
Interact with many, many people
And animals and forms of plant
Life, all of which can have a lasting
Impact on our plethora of days here
In a world so big and so enormous.

When I'm angry and feeling mad
Nothing seems to go as planned.
I get upset with everything
And I just wish my heart would sing
Thoughts of happy, thoughts of joy
Just to please this little boy.
I'm a man on the outside
While inside I want to hide
Away from this world that upsets thee
When I feel like it is out to get me.
I want to stand and scream aloud
At everyone that's in the crowd.
Oh, how I wish the world would change
And I myself could just rearrange.
I yell from the darkness and seek the light,
But it doesn't seem to be insight.
So I bow my head and turn away
From all of the colors and seek the gray.
Some day I hope I will get control
Of the world I long to console,
But I doubt that day will ever come
So I continue to stay here feeling done
With this world I've come to despise.
Maybe one day soon I'll realize
That this is something I can't fix
So I take my punches and take my licks.

Just Being With You

When You're not here
I feel so alone
I wish you'd call me
Up on the phone.

When you're not with me
Everything turns gray
I just can't stand
When I feel this way.

When I'm alone
I feel full of sadness
If you were here
I'd feel full of gladness

It's always raining
Inside of my head
I feel so sad
I wish I was dead.

I'm just feeling so lonely
I'm just feeling so blue
When you're not around
I don't know what to do.

When you're with me
I feel so alive
Just being with you
Helps me to thrive.

Just Having Some Fun

You can hear the sound
Of people everywhere
Enjoying their Tyme
And free from their cares.

Outdoors they spend Tyme
Picking fresh flowers
And sitting in the sun
As they pass the hours.

At Tymes they spend moments
In the sun at the beach
Just having fun
Isn't far out of reach.

SomeTymes they enjoy
Going for a ride
As they have some fun
Out in the countryside.

Or they have a great Tyme
Just playing with balls
While they play their sports
Spring, Summer and Fall.

Yes, they always have fun
This Tyme of the year
Just enjoying their Tyme
Our summer is here.

Just Thinking of Me

When I'm feeling blue
I don't know what to do
I want to take all my Tyme
And spend it with you.

I can try listening to music
I can talk on the phone
But nothing can help me
From feeing alone.

I can try being outside
I can try being with friends
But when you're not here
It feels like the end.

I can be surrounded by people
And yet all I feel is down
I just wish you were here
I wish you'd come back around.

So until the Tyme comes
That you're here with me
I hope that you're somewhere
Just thinking of me.

Just to Be Alive

I can hear the sound
Of bugs in the air
As they go flying
Around everywhere

And also the songs
Of birds flying, too
And of butterflies
Up in the sky so blue.

You can see some cats
And hear dogs that bark
With the sounds of children
Playing ball in the park.

You can also hear
Planes flying around
Of their take offs and landings
As they touch the ground.

The whole world is full
Of creatures that thrive
It's such a great Tyme
To just be alive.

Just Us, Two

I sit here in my leather chair,
As my cat sits beside me there.
He starts to mew as he begins to dream,
He's hoping to catch a mouse in his scheme.
He sits beside me and keeps me warm,
He knows I'll keep him safe from harm.
We make a good pair just us, two,
His purring brings me up when I'm blue.
As he sleeps his whiskers begin to twitch,
As he uses his paws to scratch an itch.
His fur is soft and his nose is wet,
Perhaps he's thinking of the treats he'll get.
Suddenly he awakens and his ears perk up,
As he goes and drinks from his water cup.
Then he goes and eats some food,
He's hoping that it will taste real good.
His fir is soft, his fur is lush,
I comb it with his favorite brush.
Then he'll sit and against me he'll lean,
He licks his fur to keep himself clean.
He lays beside me and he falls asleep.
As we sit and watch the hours to creep.
Later we'll sit and watch some T.V.
I'm so glad he spends his Tyme with me.

Keep On Going

I'm so low, I'm so low
I don't know how much lower I can go
Till I snap, Till I snap and there's no turning back.
So I cry, yes, I cry
Though I don't know just why,
I can't go on, I can't go on
But I'm trying, Yes I'm trying
Not to drown, Not to drown
In all of my sadness, In all of my sadness
In all of this mental madness.
But I'm failing, yes, I'm failing
At this game that they call life,
So I try to breathe, I try just to breathe
And hold on, and hold on with all of my might.
Yet I know, yes I know,
One day I'll be gone
And all I will have left is my writing,
But maybe some day, I'll help someone in this way
And keep them from going under.
Then all I've left behind, in my wretched mind
Are these words and my ranting and raving
Will not be for nothing.
So I say a prayer, and I try hard to care
And to continue to keep on going.

Let's Have Fun!

The day was once sunny
But now it's all gray
Still I hope we can
Hang out for the day.
We can just sit and talk
Or if you're so inclined
We could go for a walk
Just to pass the Tyme.
We could go for lunch
And have some Thai food
It really doesn't matter
As long as I'm with you.
We could have fun
By going for a ride
Just to take in
All the beauty outside.
So let's make a plan
And enjoy our little day
Before it's all gone
Let's have fun now and play!

Like I Should

I'm feeling tired and feeling lonely,
I'm tired of everyone's baloney.
I'm tired of feeling sad and blue
I'm way past tired of being used,
I'm so tired of feeling down
I'm the saddest guy in town,
I'm depressed and I'm so tired
I'm sure one day soon I'll be wired,
I'm so tired of feeling this way
I'm running out of things to say.
I'm sick of living life's extremes,
I'm ready to shout and ready to scream.
I'm living my life down in a hole,
I'm feeling like I've lost my soul.
I'm so sad and I'm so weak,
I'm feeling like a total freak.
I'm tired of watching life pass me by,
I'm so low and I don't know why.
I'm hoping one day I'll be feeling good,
I'm hoping I'll be feeling like I should.

Little Dreams

She sits here alone
With her little black kitten
Thinking of when she used
To knit gloves and mittens.
Her youth is now gone
With years now replaced
By lines and little wrinkles
All over her face.
She used to go
Down to the corner store
Just to pass the Tyme
That she had once before.
Now all of her moments
Are here in photographs
She looks at the pictures
That once made her laugh.
Now she is lonely
Her youth gone like a scheme
And all she has left
Are her sad little dreams.

He yawns as he stretches to rearrange himself in his
Little cat bed. His eyes widen and he looks all about
The room to check the status of his safety. After he
Is assured that all is clear, he gently lays back down
And falls into sleep again. His paws twitch as do his
Ears checking for signs of other life going on all around
Him. He yawns again and his little nose scrunches up
Too. He peers all around the room and takes a look
At what is going on around him. When he is sure that
It is safe, he curls up into his bed again and falls asleep.
After a while he wakes and begins his morning routine
Of washing himself. He starts with his two front legs
And then his two back legs and then finally his tail is
Groomed for the remainder of the day. He looks all
Around the room and decides that all is clear and safe
And then he falls gently back to sleep as the rest of the
World goes on around him.

Love makes the world go round and round,
Love is the greatest emotion around.
Love is the best thing when you're feeling blue,
Love is the celebration of hearts for two.
Love is emotion without limits,
Love is the best when you are in it.
Love is the best when you spend it together,
Love is in bloom despite the weather.
Love is great, love is pure,
Love is the depression's cure.
Love is darkness turned to light,
Love will make you feel alright.
Love is the best way to show you care,
Love is the greatest way to share.
Love is the heart set in motion,
Love is known as the heart's devotion.
Love is bright, love is red,
Love is your heart inside your head.
Love is as gentle as a SpringTyme shower,
Love is a nice bouquet of flowers.
Love is shown best with a kiss,
Love is the true emotion of bliss.
Love is the emotion shared by a friend
Love is all there is in the end.

Love's Reflection

Your Love lifts me so high
I feel like I could touch the sky,
Your Love makes me feel so whole
I feel like I could touch your soul.

When we are just us two together
I feel so good despite the weather,
When we're alone at night
I know your Love makes everything alright.

Your Love makes me feel so grand
I feel the need to touch your hand,
Your eyes they shine so bright
I know your Love's reflected in their light.

When you say the nice things to me
I know that my heart is finally free,
When you say the things you do
I know that your Love is true.

Low

SomeTymes I just feel so blue,
I don't know just what to do.
I don't know just what to say,
To keep me from feeling this way.
SomeTymes I just feel so low,
I don't know how much further I can go.
I have to look up to see down,
On my face I wear a frown.
Most Tymes I feel so alone,
I can't get anyone on the phone.
SomeTymes I just wish I'd die,
Life just gets so hard to try.
I can get so damned depressed,
Life just makes me feel so stressed.
When I'm alone all I do is cry,
Though I'm not sure just why.
I don't know just what to say,
To help keep me from feeling this way.
SomeTymes I wish I wouldn't wake,
Feeling this way is hard to take.
I wonder if my friends miss me
Because I'm as lonely as can be.
Some days I hope to see my friends again,
Then maybe again my mind will mend.

Mom 2

I Love my mom, she is the best,
She's better than all of the rest.
I have Loved her from the start,
She has got a golden heart.
I think that she's like the sun,
She shines bright on everyone.
I like spending Tyme with her,
She can make good things occur.
I like talking with her on the phone,
She keeps me company when I'm alone.
I always have fun when we get together,
She always smiles despite the weather.
I know she's funny and always witty,
She always looks nice, she always looks pretty.
She is the nicest person I know,
She makes me feel better when I'm feeling low.
I know she's more precious than silver or gold,
She make me feel young, even though I'm old.
In spite of whether we're near or far,
We always have a good Tyme wherever we are.

Monarch

Out in the yard
There's a monarch butterfly
That goes from leaf to leaf,
Just trying to find its place
In a world so large and cold.
It flaps its wings there
All alone in the sun.
I can't even imagine
What it must be like
To be so small and tiny
In a place as big as this.
Its Tyme on this planet
Restricted to a mere
Number of days
Instead of years and
Decades. Thinking like
This makes me realize
How very, very lucky
We are to be big people
In a big, big space.

Monster

You went out a man,
And came home a monster...
Each and every Tyme you went out.
There was no rhyme or reason
For the way that always you acted.
You drank till you were completely insane.
Then out came the claws and the your teeth
Gnashing and biting the air and with the words
That you chose. You could spew them out faster
Than the speed of light, cursing words that a child
Should never hear, let alone repeat them.
Then you took the stage and began your
Frantic frolics. That's when the real you began
To shine on through: breaking things just for the fun of it.
And when all was said and done you stalked off to the bedroom
Where you would finally crash and burn and sleep till the next day.
Then you would start it all over again...Repeat...Repeat...Repeat...
Repeat.

My Best Friend

You're a true friend and it always shows,
You're always so kind, that's the way it goes.
I Love to spend Tyme with you, you make me laugh,
I know that we're two parts and you're my better half.
You know that I Love you, I would do anything
I'm just so proud to wear your ring.
We enjoy each other, we have such fun,
We're two friends together, you warm me like the sun.
I want to tell you just how much you mean to me,
You're the kind of soul that sets me free.
You help bring me up when I am blue,
You always say the right thing, you know it's true,
We can spend hours doing nothing at all,
We're there for each other Winter, Spring, Summer or Fall.
I think of you as my best friend,
I know you'll be there for me until the end.

My Day With You

The air is fresh,
The sky is blue,
It's the kind of day
I'd like to spend with you.
We can go out for a walk,
From when it's dawn
Till it gets dark.
We could go down by the lake,
And have a picnic
With sandwiches and cake.
We could share a bit of wine,
You know for sure
We'll have a good Tyme.
We can bring the radio along,
So we can hear some of our favorite songs.
Maybe we could catch some fish,
Or skip some stones
And make a wish.
It doesn't matter
What we do,
As long as I can spend
My day with you.

My Mom

She's the nicest person that I know,
She's got a heart that's pure as gold.
She's so nice, she's so sweet,
Spending Tyme with her is such a treat.
She always make what's wrong alright,
She's is always my guiding light.
She's more than a mom, she's my best friend,
She will be with me till the end.
She brings me up when I'm alone,
She talks to me each day by phone.
She's a little piece of heaven
She's more than a ten, she's an eleven.
She's very smart, she's so wise,
She never gives in, she always tries.
She's got a sense of humor, she's so witty,
She always looks nice, she always looks pretty,
She's always kind, she's the best,
She always shines above the rest.

My Teddy Bear

You are my teddy bear, no bones about it…
I feel your big teddy arms around me when
You give me a hug or when you hold onto
Me. You have those big shoulders and chest
And I can feel them when you wrap them
Around me at night when we are snuggling.
Like the bear that you are, you give to me
That great big smile that is eternally happy.
I hope that the reason that you are so calm
And content is because you are thinking
About us together. Those big brown eyes
Of yours are the best feature on your face.
Those big brown eyes say "I Love you" in
Oh, so many ways. I am in Love with
Everything those handsome and attractive
Peepers have to say to me. Finally there
Are your big bear paws. I Love nothing
More than to hold your hand in mine till
The end of Tyme. I am truly in Love with
You my Loving teddy bear.

My True Love Shines

Today I dreamt of my true Love
I knew he'd been sent from heaven above,
I think of the many years we've had
So many days were good and a few were bad,
I recalled the days spent in his arms
Entranced by his good looks and charms,
I so enjoyed looking in his brown eyes
I was so happy that he was all mine,
I enjoy just sitting within his arms around me
At these Tymes I knew what heaven can mean,
We spent all of our free Tyme together
He makes me smile despite the weather,
He always makes me feel adored
As he keeps me company when I am bored,
We often enjoy just holding hands
As we walk on the beach in the warm sand,
He has the power to make me sing
I know how to fly without any wings,
He helps me to feel Loved and fight my strife
I am so very lucky to have him in my life.

Shadow lays napping in his bed. While
He was napping he opens his eyes once
And a while and takes in all that is going
On around him. While he falls into a
Deeper sleep, he begins to dream. As
He dreams he makes a snoring sound.
I would Love to know what he dreams
About. Perhaps mice? Maybe running
Free outdoors? Then suddenly as I am
Watching him, he opens his eyes and
He becomes aware and alert of all of
His surroundings. Then as quickly as
He awoke, he falls back to sleep. As
He lays there, his ears begin to perk
Up as he searches the room for sounds
And he slowly falls gently back to sleep.

No Matter Near or Far

When I think of you it just blows my mind,
We get along so well 'cause you're so kind.
We've come so far after all these years,
You make me feel safe… you calm my fears.
When we're together we have such fun,
Your smile it shines just like the sun.
When we're together the Tyme just flies,
If I'm with you I know it's safe to cry.
We're there for each other…come what may,
You're here for me in each and every way.
I save up my Love and I save it just for you,
You make me feel happy with all that you do.
When I am lost, you help me find my way home.
We stick together, no matter where we roam.
If you need me, you need only call my name,
It's true for you… I know you feel the same.
I'm here for no matter wherever you're near or far,
I Love you just the way you are.

No Regrets

With every thought and with every breath
I get a little closer to my impending death.
My life gets shorter with each move I make
And every heartbeat and every step I take
I'm getting closer and closer to my end
And trying to get myself to now mend.
I try to fix things to the way they used to be
Trying to figure out what I'm supposed to see.
I sit and watch the sky go from dark to bright
As I slowly begin to pray now for the light.
I pray to God with every thing that I do
So I may have another day here with you.
With each moment I thank God for the chance
To share our Love and share our romance.
Perhaps the sun will shine again once more
As I step one step closer to the final door.
So please God hear me calling to you now
And help me make it through somehow,
For when all is over and said and done
I will have no regrets, not a single one.

No Smile On My Face

I'm feeling down, I'm feeling low
I know there isn't much farther down I can go.
I have to look up just to see down,
All I have on my face is a frown.
I'm feeling sad, I'm feeling depressed,
If I thought about it more I'd be obsessed.
I don't know why I must live this way,
I wish I could just run away.
I'm feeling sad, I'm feeling tired
I feel like my expiration date has expired.
I'm so low, I'm so blue
I wish I knew just what to do.
There's no smile on my face,
I feel like I'm alone in space.
I've lost my heart, I've lost my mind
This world has me feeling so unkind.
Who is at fault, who is to blame,
I'm so lost I can't remember my name
I can't sleep, I only cry
I wish I could find a hole in which to die.
I'm so lost, I'm so alone,
A house without you is not a home

Christmas is over,
The New Year's begun,
It's Tyme to rejoice
It's Tyme to have fun.
So put away all the decorations
And put away the tree,
Those old days are over,
It's Tyme to break free.
Outside it is cold,
Outside there is snow,
We leave footprints behind
Where ever we go.
So dust off the toboggan,
And dust off your skates,
Get outside and enjoy the weather,
It'll make you feel great.
If you get cold
Try some hot chocolate
It'll make you feel bold.
So get out your skis
And don't you be late
Enjoy the wintry weather,
There's no Tyme to wait.

On Death and Dying

SomeTymes when we least expect it, we lose a
Friend when they pass on from this world to the
Next. We can be caught off guard and left to
Wonder why someone dies when they are so
Young and so vibrant and full of life. When
This happens we ask ourselves why did this
Occur…This happened to me recently and I
Am still wondering "Why?". My friend was
In her forties and she always seemed so lively
And bubbly. I asked myself over and over if
There wasn't something I could have done to
Prepare myself for this occurrence. As humans,
We all deal with death in different ways. Often
We are saddened and feel a loss in a way that
Makes us wonder if there is a reason for the
Loss that we just aren't seeing at the Tyme.
SomeTymes we feel angry at a loss when
There seems to be no reason for an unTymely
Death. This leads to questions and a family
Struggling to get through a difficult situation.
It is at these Tymes that turning to God is the
Only way we can get through the ordeal and
Survive the sadness it has left us feeling.

On Getting Older

One of the nicest things I've noticed about getting
Older is that things that used to bother you so much
When you were younger, don't seem to get you all
Rattled up like they did when you were very young.
You learn that life is way too short to spend it all riled
Up. You learn that as you get into your older set of
Decades of years. Life goes way too fast and that if
You spend it hanging on to needless little details you
Are really only wasting Tyme that could better be
Used for more important things. Conversely, when
You get older you realize some of the best parts of
Life are the little things that you took for granted
When you were younger. One of the best parts of
Getting older is the wonderful things like nature and
Life in general have more meaning like the one thing
That you took for granted is with your relationship with
Your significant other and your relationship with what
You deem as your higher power. As you get older
You seek stronger friendships in people and with nature
Such as animals and spiritual relationships. Put quite
Simply, you don't sweat the small stuff anymore.

On the Outside

Outside the wind rips through the air. The air
Temperature is in the negative digits. I can't
Help but think that it is a perfect day for the
Penguins and polar bears. It is most definitely
A day to stay inside where the air is warm and
Cozy. As I look around the room I see my many
House plants that couldn't survive in weather
Such as this. I like the weather when it is
Between cool and warm, somewhere around
Sixty and seventy degrees. I don't like having
To put on lots of layers to stay warm, but rather
Clothes that just keep you comfortable and
Content. Here in Wisconsin, you get a Winter
That goes from November until March, some-
Tymes a little longer if you aren't lucky. The
Best Tyme of the year is from May until the
End of September. I have often wondered
Why people choose to live in a place where
It is so cold for much of the year. I think it
Is because they like the changing of the
Seasons. There are also those folks who like
The Winter sports as well as the Summer ones.
I, myself like the Winter sports as well, I just
Enjoy observing them from the distance of a
Nice warm couch.

Our Day Together

It's the perfect day
To cut the lawn,
While I play some tunes
And sing along.
Or maybe we
Could wash the car,
And make it shine
Like the evening star.
We could take a walk
Down to the park,
And sit and swing
Till it gets dark.
We could sit
Out in the sun,
And have a drink
To have some fun.
We could go
Down by the pool,
And splash around
To keep us cool.
It's such a nice day,
It's perfect weather,
To get to spend
Our day together.

Pressing Palms

When everything's not going right,
Turn from the darkness and seek His light.
Put your faith in God above,
Press your palms and pray for His Love.
If you falter, He will catch your fall,
He Loves everyone and all.
When you're down and feeling weak,
Let Him be the one you seek.
He rules over all the Earth,
Let him fill your heart with Love and mirth.
His kingdom is heaven in the sky,
He rules where the angels fly.
He will hear the prayers you say
When you press your palms and pray.
Over everything he comes first,
Any place can be your church.
He can hear you from anywhere
He will always treat you fair.
He will hold you in his hand,
He is king of every land.
Always keep Him in your heart,
He can make the seas to part.
He is great and He is good,
He will surely lift your mood.
To the Earth, he gave his son
God is king of everyone.

Rainbows

Rainbows, those colorful collection of lights after a
Storm, can always put a smile on your face. The
Bright shades of color can put a lift to your day...
Even if the day wasn't so nice to begin with. They
Have us all wondering if there really is a pot of
Gold at the end of its shiny tail. Maybe it's because
We want to believe that just maybe we will be the
One to find it and collect up all the gold for our-
Selves. Maybe, just maybe that shiny trail of lights
Can bring a bit of magic to our day. After all, who
Doesn't like a bit of magic now and then? Magic...
Just enough to bring a smile to the doubters among
Us. The colors can bring a drop or two of tears of
Joy, just enough to make us all believe in those
Colorful waves of light. For those who believe,
They know that there will never again be a flood
That will wash us all away. Rainbows shine all the
Colors of the palette with just enough light to remind
Us that all of colors are just as important as the ones
That we are: red, yellow, black and white. Colors,
Bright shiny colors that can bring a bit of hope to
An otherwise dark and weary world.

Sad

I'm feeling sad and depressed today,
I wish I didn't feel this way.
Living life can be so rough,
It forces you to be tough.
I never felt like I fit in,
I wouldn't want to live again.
I would choose another life,
One that has far less strife.
When I get depressed, I get tired,
And when I get manic I get wired.
It's a messed up way to live,
I wish that I had more in life to give.
My life is such an awful mess,
And to this I must confess,
I'm so tired of feeling down,
On my face I wear a frown.
Some days all I do is cry,
When I do I wish I'd die,
SomeTymes it makes me so mad,
It makes me tired of feeling sad.
I'm so tired of taking pills,
I just wish they'd cure my ills.
Some days I wish that I was dead,
It's hard to live inside my head.

Santa's Here

It's the holiday Tyme
And Christmas is near,
People are shopping
They're all full of cheer,
They're ready for Christmas
Santa's on his way,
He'll be bearing gifts
Upon Christmas day,
Children are excited
They can hardly sleep,
They're waiting for Santa
They won't make a peep,
They're waiting for presents
He'll deliver them soon,
He'll be with his reindeer
As he flies past the moon,
He'll come down the chimney
Bearing gifts for one and all,
For children of all ages
Short, big, tall and small,
So make sure you leave him
Some cookies to eat,
He may just be hungry
And in need of a treat,
And when he leaves
Up the chimney he'll go
Onto the next family
With his bags of gifts all in tow.

Goodnight my sweet Jesus
And his Father God on high,
I wish that I could join you
In your kingdom in the sky.
I'd leave behind all I know
And everything it's worth,
So I could live in heaven
And leave behind the earth.
In heaven it is peaceful
And everyone is kind,
In contrast to a warring world
That's destructive to the mind
So hear me my lord Jesus
I'm running out of Tyme
Please take me up to heaven
Where everything's sublime.

Scars

The battle is long since over, and all that remains
Are the scars that you left behind on me…So, so
Many scars left behind and how they came to be.
All those scars that you left behind on me and how
They came to be…Oh, those scars, you left behind
On me and how they came to be. All those scars,
The ones that you left behind on me, without even
Noticing the carnage and twisted path you'd made.
My mind is all torn up in the torment because of
The intensity at which you go squealing through
The day, and all I can do is to hold on, and on,
And on. Your overzealous ways will surely be
The end of me. And by far the last thing that you
Speak, God knows that I tried to be the one the
One that you wanted me to be. I know that you
Are so enamored with yourself, (Just like you to
Be the one who runs the show and still does!).
But you are wrong in oh, so many ways and it is
Tyme for you to finally meet your maker. Under
Your scars you're nothing but a washed up loser…
And this will never change. Now it is Tyme for
Me to leave one once and for all with you, just
You, just you! Oh, this scar I leave behind on
You, I leave behind on you, sums it all up to a
Finish…WE ARE THROUGH!!

Shadow's Sleepy Tyme

Shadow sleeps alone in his little bed. He sleeps there
During the better part of the afternoon. As he sleeps
I can hear the subtle sound of his snoring as he dreams
His little dreams. Every once in a while he turns over
And finds a new way to continue his dreaming. I often
Wonder just what he dreams about. Does he dream of
Exploring the great out doors or does he dream about
Me playing with him by his side? Every once on a
While his ears will twitch back and forth. His body
Will rearrange itself in his cat bed. It's funny how he
Will sleep away the greater part of the day and spend
The entire evening rustling about the rooms and checking
On everything. His legs move around as he finds a new
Position to sleep in. Ever so slightly his chest rises and
Falls. He is oblivious to all things going on around him
As he continues his cat nap. His gentle purring is telling
Me that he feels secure enough in his surroundings to
Sleep away the afternoon. Being nocturnal, he rests
Away the daytyme hours and stores up his energy so as
To be ready to begin his exploration of the house when
The evening settles in. It is then that he searches the
Rooms for mice as the rest of the world settles in for
A long night sleep.

Show Me Some Love

I'm feeling bad, I'm feeling blue,
There's not much more that I can do,
To make it through this state I'm in,
I need some help, I need a friend.
I put my faith in God above,
This situation's gone from push to shove.
God Knows I'm feeling down today,
He surely knows all I feel is pain.
I hope some day I'll be feeling better,
I'm so sick of this nasty weather.
I put my faith in the Lord above,
My situation's gone from push to shove.
All I feel is blue today,
There's nothing more for me to say.
I feel I've come to my life's end,
I wish I had a real good friend.
I put my faith in God above,
This situation's gone from push to shove.
Please help me God, please help me through,
There's not much more that I can do.
To make it through this state I'm in
I feel like God's my only friend.
I put my faith in the Lord above,
My situation's gone from push to shove.
So I put my faith in God above,
I put my faith in God above,
I put my faith in God above,
I put my faith in God above,
Please help me God, show me some Love.

Skinner

One day at the tender age of five,
I walked in on my father and uncles
Skinning a deer that they had gone and hunted.
They were peeling the fur and skin down,
The body hanging from a rope in the garage ceiling.
I was so scared I went completely numb
And I couldn't move a single muscle…
Suddenly, my mother burst into the scene
As she knew what was going on in there.
She grabbed me and covered my eyes,
But it was too late. I had seen the majestic animal
Being stripped of its hide, skin and fur.
That one small incident caused me severe
Distress in the near future. In my eyes
I could recall that scene over and over
In my nightmares for many years to come.
It was about as horrific as you can possibly
Imagine. As a child I Loved all animals
And I couldn't in any way understand how
My father and uncles could be part of such a
Brutal scene. It wasn't that they had killed
An innocent animal as timid as a deer, but
That they had hanged the deer from the ceiling
Of our garage, but that they had proceeded to
Pull the skin off of the deer. Blood, skin and
Dead animal…it is definitely not something
A very young child should see…EVER.
It was enough to cause myself to never, ever
Kill any of God's creatures big or small for
The rest of my entire life!

Sleep Tyme

Many years ago, when I was still in high school,
I used to have trouble sleeping. SomeTymes I
Would just lay in bed trying to get back to sleep.
Other Tymes, I would get dressed and go to the
Park across from my house and just swing on
The swings trying to calm myself down and get
Back to sleep. That park was the place where I
Had some of my best memories as a child growing
Up. It was very comforting to know that I could
Just swing for as much Tyme as I needed to get
Back to sleep. Often, when I was swinging I
Would someTymes stare up at skies and just
Look up at the stars. The sight of the stars was
Very relaxing to me and I would think of all of
The wonderful planets and stars that were out
There in space just waiting to be discovered. I
Would pretend that I was an astronaut that was
The one who was discovering new forms of life
And bringing them back to earth to become a
Part of our planets many different types of beings.
SomeTymes I was just swinging for hours just
Trying to get back to sleep and hoping I could
Get the sleep I so desperately needed.

Outside the snowflakes fall gently to the ground.
Eventually enough falls so as to cover the outside
World in white. Throughout the day more snow
Falls and the covering gets to be enough to carpet
The world in a white blanket of calm and gentle
Softness. As the day progresses, little tracks are
Left behind on the snowfall revealing that there
Is a whole other world moving about throughout
The day. Under the white layer of grass and
Shrubs continue their slumber for the greater part
Of the winter. I am never ceased to be amazed
At how the cold hard ground is still alive through
The winter when there is no rain or sun shine to
Keep it going and only frigid temperatures that
Continue for the months of Winter. Nothing that
Is human could survive the onslaught of cold for
So many months without water and the need for
Food that the sunlight provides for the plant world
During the other seasons of the year. Wouldn't it
Be wonderful if our human race could hibernate
The entire Winter like the plants and trees do?
We could store up our energy for four or five
Months of Winter and save it for the joyous return
Of the Spring through the Fall months when the
Warmth of the sun returns.

Outside the cold winter wind blows all about. People
Stay indoors where it is nice and warm and dry. As I
Look back in Tyme to years gone by, I remember how
We would spend hours and hours outside building a
Snow fort and a snow family. I would spend the entire
Day just playing in the deep, deep snow. Later we
Would come inside for some hot chocolate and warm
Up before going back outdoors for more fun in the
Snow. It is funny how as you get older you seem to
Like being less outside with friends and playing in the
Winter mix. As you get older you want to be inside
Where it is warm and toasty. As I got older, I seemed
To spend more tyme skating and skiing, never worrying
About the consequences of falling and hurting myself.
These days I would be afraid I might fall and break a hip
If I wasn't careful. Today I don't like being outside any
More than is necessary, but I still enjoy a nice cup of nice
Hot chocolate.

Somehow

Dear God, up in heaven
I'm pleading with you now,
Please help me make it through somehow.
My God up in heaven
I fear I'm coming apart.
Please help me heal my broken heart.
While my heart is mending
I say thanks to you...
I say it with a heart that speaks full true.
So, God high up in heaven
I'm begging you now,
Please help me to make it through this
Help me make it through somehow.

Summer Vacation

When I was a young boy
I had a heart filled with joy,
I enjoyed playing ball
In Spring, Summer and Fall,
I would play at the park
From dawn until dark,
We built castles made of sand
That made us feel grand,
We played with our toys
That filled us with joy,
We would go to the beach
And swim in the water so deep,
It was always so fun
Just to play in the sun,
SomeTymes we went hiking
And other Tymes we went biking,
A picnic lunch was a treat
And so much fun to eat,
We'd fish off the pier
In the water so clear,
We had fun catching frogs
And playing with our dogs,
Yes, we'd play with our friends
In a summer that never ends.

Summer's Finally Here

The weather is nice
The weather is fair
The butterflies are flying
In the fresh Spring air.

And too the flowers
Are starting to bloom
Like they always do
In the month of June.

The wind is blowing
Through all of the leaves
The birds are making nests
Up high in the trees.

Soon the nests will be
Full of baby birds
While their parents sing
Their songs without words.

Outdoors are the kids
Enjoying the weather
While they run around
And play games together.

Outside are the folks
Down by the pool
As they enjoy Tyme
Away from their school.

The days are long
This Tyme of the year
It's so fun to play
Summer's finally here.

Survive

Without friends it's hard to survive,
These days it's hard just to stay alive.
SomeTymes life can be so rough.
It forces you to be tough.
How I miss my childhood friends,
On them, how I did depend.
Oh, where are they now?
I sure miss them anyhow.
They were always good to me,
They helped to set my soul free.
We always had a real good Tyme.
To lose them feels just like a crime.
It makes me to feel alone,
When I can't get them on the phone,
I wish they were still in my life,
Without them my life's full of strife.
We used to have so much fun,
Without them I feel so numb.
I miss those good old days together,
While through the bad Tymes we did weather.
Without friends life just feels so lame,
I wonder if they'll remember my name.

Take Me Away

Take me away to where the skies are blue,
And the grass is always so green,
It's the nicest place that you've ever seen...
Take me away to where the people are always friendly,
And the pets are too,
There's so many things for you to do
All you need is to be yourself,
Leave your depression up on the shelf.
All you need is to smile today
Send your sadness upon it's way.
Life is so good, the Tymes are too
No more Tyme for feeling blue.
Take me away to where it never rains,
And the sun always shines again.
It's the perfect place to leave your sadness behind,
The people are friendly, and the pets are too
There's lots of things for you to do.
All you need is to be yourself
Leave your depression up on the shelf.
All you need is to smile today,
Send your sadness on it's way.
Life is good, the Tymes are too
No you won't be feeling blue,
Oh, no you won't be feeling blue again
It's the nicest place you've ever been.
Yes, it's the nicest place you've ever been.
It's the nicest place you've ever been.

Thank You So Much

I'm feeling so sad
It's a mess in my head
When I'm all alone
I feel like I'm dead.

I feel so lonely
As I sit here and cry
Just feeling this way
Makes me wish I would die.

The weather is sunny
In my head I feel blue
I'd feel much better
If I was with you

Yes, you bring me up
When we get together
You help me feel happy
In spite of the weather.

To make things alright
Call me on the phone
It's so much better
Than being alone.

When you're with me
Everything turns bright
Thank you so much
For making things right.

Thankful

Life is very short…no doubt about that. I have learned
Over the years that it is not always what you say that
Counts, but how you say it that carries a heavy weight.
One of the easiest ways to make someone's day is to
Just thank them for the things that they do for you that
Matters. By saying something positive, you can change
The whole scope of your conversations. Another thing
To do that is nice is to remind someone how grateful
You are to have them in your life. Complimenting some-
One on their hairstyle or clothing is a great way to make
Someone's day. The nice thing about complimenting
Someone is that it is a great game changer. When you
Talk with someone, you never really know how their
Day was up to that point in the day. If their day has
Not been going well, a simple comment can change the
Course of day and it doesn't cost you anything either.
Being nice to others is a great way to change their day
As well as yours. So the next Tyme you come across
Someone, do the right thing and say something nice
For a change. They will surely appreciate it.

The Deep, Deep Snow

The weather is cold, the snow is deep
It's a place where the Tyme just creeps,
Don't feel bad if you feel sad today,
Send all of your sadness on it's way.
No, you won't be feeling sad again,
As now the snow turns into rain.
The weather is cold, the snow piled high,
It's a place where the Tyme just flies.
Don't feel bad if you feel sad today,
Send all your sadness on it's way.
No, you won't be feeling sad again,
As the snow turns into rain.
Soon the days of Spring will be here,
As the weather turns from cloudy to clear.
Don't feel bad if you feel sad today,
Send all of your sadness on it's way.
No, you won't be feeling sad again,
Because the snow is turning to rain.
The weather is starting to get good
You'll soon be feeling like you should.
No, you won't be feeling sad today,
All of your sadness has washed away.
No more feeling sad again,
Because the snow has turned to rain.
No more feeling sad and blue,
How you feel is up to you.
No more feeling sad again,
The snow has finally turned to rain.

The Falling Rain

The rain falls slowly from the clouds
And when it does it hits the ground.
It makes a splatter here and there
It makes the ground wet everywhere.
The rain helps the plants to grow
When it's cold rain turns to snow.
The rain helps the world to thrive
Because water keeps us all alive.
It's fun to jump in big rain puddles
While under an umbrella we cuddle.
When it storms we see the lightning
Sounds of thunder can be frightening.
We hear sounds when thunder storms
While indoors we stay safe and warm.

She say quietly in her rocking chair on the porch of
Her house. She began to reminisce about the days
When she was much younger and still in school.
She remembered her friends from school and how
They would play at one another's homes. She
Loved how they would play with their dolls and their
Friends. They liked to pretend that they were much
Older and that they had a big family to take care of.
They liked to name their dolls after their friends.
She loved playing the role of the mother and they
Would feed their dolls and give them a bottle of
Milk. One of her favorite names was Sandy. She
Chose that name because it was the name of a
Celebrity that she liked. She would play for many
Hours until her older brothers showed up and began
To tease the girls. One of their favorite things to
Play was that they were at school and that she was
The teacher. They liked to take chalk and write on
The sidewalk and play out their lessons. Years later
She still remembered how much she missed her
Good friends from her childhood. They were some
Of the best friends that she ever had.

The Gully

Growing up in Portage, Wisconsin, I was
Fond of a little park called the Gully
Where we would go to fish in the little pond
And where we'd go to skate in the winter Tyme.
There was a group of trails that surrounded
The pond and an area where we would go
To play kickball and softball. There was
Even a little area where we would play
On an outdoor jungle gym. There was an
Enclosed area where we would meet with
A park and recreations group instructor
And make arts and crafts items that we
Could make for free. The best part about
It was that all the other parks in town also
Had summer recreations going on as well
So you could go to the park nearest you
And meet and play every day on Mondays
Through Fridays with the kids that lived
Nearby. The instructors were high school
Kids who wanted to oversee the activities
That went on during the days and were there
To make sure all went smooth and the kids
All got along. I was lucky enough to be
Between two different parks: Lincoln Park
And the Gully. There was never a day that
Went by without something fun going on.
It was truly the best part of summer vacation.

The Perfect Day

I look up to the sky
As I see clouds roll by.
I see some geese and a loon.
It is a great afternoon.
I step into the light
The temperature feels just right.
It's just a wonderful day.
Summer is on its way.
I turn and walk outside.
It's Tyme to go for a ride.
I hear the songs of birds
As they speak without words.
I smell the fresh clean air,
There are people everywhere.
There are people on the street.
They smile at the folks they meet.
I see people outside walking.
I can tell that they are talking.
There's nothing that I'd rather do
Than spend my day with you.
Let's go and sit in the sun.
It's the perfect day for everyone.

The Perfect Ending

Up in the sky, the clouds are beginning to come
Together and fill it up with rain clouds. The air
Starts to cool off and I can feel I slight chill in
The air as the sky darkens to an overcast horizon.
As I stand outside I can begin to feel the drops
Of rain as they begin to fall. At first there is only
A light sprinkle, but slowly the droplets begin to
Fall faster and in a few moments the rain begins
To fall. I can see the droplets hitting the ground
And making the sidewalk wet. The rain falls
Rapidly now and the grass is wet and soggy.
The smell of rain permeates the air. I just sit
On the porch and watch the rain fall. The air
Temperature cools and it feels just right. The
Sound of the rain relaxes me and I listen to the
Sound of the thunder in the distance. After an
Hour the clouds have rained themselves out and
The storm comes to an end. Somewhere in the
Sky the clouds part and reveal the wonderful
Sight of a rainbow appears. The perfect ending
To a perfect storm.

The Season of Caring and Sharing

The lights on the tree
Fill us with glee,
The scent of the pine
Smells so divine,
Christmas sweets and candies
Taste oh, so dandy,
Sledding on the snow
Leaves our faces all aglow,
Christmas carols and songs
Make us all want to sing along,
A hot Christmas meal
Can fill us with zeal,
Skating on ponds of ice
Is always quite nice,
Christmas presents and toys
Fills our hearts full of joy,
A Christmas vacation
Leaves us with elation,
Christmas cookies and pies
Can light up our eyes,
A warm Christmas sweater
Will make us feel better,
The Christmas star in the night
Will always shine bright,
Santa and his deer
Fill children with cheer,
Christmas logs all afire
Fills our hearts with desire
And Jesus Christ is the reason
We celebrate the season.

The Stars Above

The stars are pretty,
The stars are bright,
I'm making my wish
On the stars tonight.
And when I wish
I'm wishing for you,
And forever I hope
My dreams will come true.
I'll make a wish
That we'll stay together,
And that it will be
That way forever.
I made my wish
And it was for Love,
I'm forever thankful
To the stars above.

The Sun

The sun is always shining so bright
As it fills the world up with it's light.
The sun gives us light all day,
As it sends darkness on its way.
The sun makes us all feel nice and warm
It always shines brightly after storm.
The sun shines the world around,
And it shines without a sound.
The sun keeps the plants alive,
It also helps the world to thrive.
The sun gives us our vitamin D,
It fills the world with light for free.
The sun rises in the east and settles in the west,
The sun always makes us all look our best.
The sun always makes the grass grow green,
As leaves behind a shadow where it's been.
The sun shines brightest when it is noon,
At night it helps to light up the moon.
The sun is really 5 billion years old,
It shines in beautiful shades of gold.
The sun makes the background sky look blue,
Isn't that a wonderful thing to do?

I'm feeling down and sad today,
It seems so often that I feel this way.
Nothing seems to fix my mood,
From feeling bad to feeling good.
I take my meds, yes I take my pills,
Still I'm feeling sad and ill.
The days go slowly, the nights are long,
Every little thing I do goes wrong.
Please help me God, to make things right,
I'm trying hard with all my might.
I'm feeling sad, I'm feeling alone,
My mind is wandering far from home.
Nothing seems to fix my mood,
From feeling bad to feeling good.
I take my meds, yes I take my pills,
Still I'm feeling sad and ill.
The days go slowly, the nights are long,
Every little thing I do goes wrong.
Please help me God, to make things right,
I try so hard to keep up this fight.
Maybe one day I'll be feeling better,
I can't take much more of this weather.
Maybe one day soon I'll be feeling better,
Please help me God, to make it through this weather.

Good To Be Free

I'm sitting on the couch outside
Just taking in all of the sounds,
The day is warm and bright
My happiness all abounds.
I'm watching all of the birds,
It is good to be outdoors,
I can see them everywhere,
I'm looking for some more.
Staring at the blue skies,
I'm watching a jet stream trail,
The trail goes on and on
The jets are flying without fail.
Looking at the green lawn
The weather is warm and fair,
There are so many little, bugs,
They are flying everywhere.
I'm looking at the clouds
The skies are teeming with life,
There are life forms everywhere,
They are flying without strife.
I'm taking in the trees today
The buds are popping all over,
They're just growing leaves,
The grass is full of clover.
I'm staring at the heavens
Hoping God is watching over me,
He oversees everything,
It feels so good to be free.

Days Without Rain

Here I am the one and only,
Today I just feel oh, so lonely.
The weather outside is cold and bad
This kind of weather can make you sad.
Looking outside the sky is gray,
I wish the clouds would go away.
As I step outside to get the mail,
The weather makes me feel old and frail
So I stay inside next to my cat,
He eats too much and now he's fat.
When I'm on the couch he sits next to me.
He has black fur and he's cute as can be.
When he's asleep he'll start to purr,
Then he moves and begins to stir.
He wishes he could go outside.
Where there's lots of places to hide.
He likes to watch the birds out there
Where they are flying without a care.
Some day soon we'll sit in the sun
Where he can catch some birds for fun.
Here's hoping we can get together
When we have a day without bad weather
Someday soon we'll have no rain
And we can get outside again.

To Fly

I see the sun up in the sky,
It makes me wish that I could fly.
I'd fly straight up in the air,
I'd fly without even a care.
I'd fly just like the birds do,
I'd fly up in the heavens with you.
I'd fly just to be free,
I'd fly just to see what I can see.
I'd fly just to look down at the ground,
I'd fly high and never come down.
So if you want to fly way up in the sky,
So if you want to give it a try,
Come and set you soul free,
Come and fly up there with me.

I sit here feeling alone and sad
At a great big world that makes me mad.
Oh, so many things that I would change
If I could make it rearrange.
I'd stop the world from all the wars
And hope we get to fix them some more.
I would make the folks to get along
And I'd try to fix to right its wrongs.
I would teach the world to sing
And bring forth the Love it brings
I would make right all of our mistakes
And stop the world from all its aches.
I would teach the world to Love
And find its faith in God above.
There are so many wrongs that I'd make right
And take them forth to seek the light.

Until the Very End

When I get down I think of you
If I am sad it gets me through,
I just think of your smiling face
Then my blues are gone without a trace,
I see your smile, I see your eyes
I Love you because you're so wise,
The things you say make me feel better
You're my sunshine despite bad weather,
I take your hand and hold it in mine
It always makes me feel so fine,
You lift me up to touch the sky
And when you do I feel so high,
When you hold me in your arms
I know you'll keep me safe from harm,
The night will end with just a kiss
It puts me in a state of bliss,
When I need you I need only call
You always catch me when I fall,
Of all my friends, you are my best
You always shine above the rest.
Oh, I'm so glad you're my best friend
We will be together until the end.

Very Soon By My Side

When you were here
Our Love grew like ivy
Now nothing grows
When you're not beside me
Tyme lingers on
I feel so alone
Nothing feels right
When you're not at home.
Because when you're near
All seemed so much better
All I feel is blue
When we're not together
Give Love one more chance
To make things alright
I'm hoping to see you
Very soon by my side.

What Great Luck

As I look into your eyes, I see the Love that I feel
For you reflected back to me. Your big smile says
That you feel the same way that I do. Staring into
Those eyes, I feel the kindness that I do for you, as
Well as the rest of your family. You don't need to say
A word because I know just what you are thinking.
I take your hand in mine and feel the strength of
The Love we share for one another. As we look
Into the sky, we are both awestruck by the number
Of stars that we can see from where we are sitting.
We are both so very lucky to have found each other
In a world so big as the one in which we both live
In. We are two very lucky people to have found
Love in an often cold world and to have maintained
A friendship as well as a marriage. As we come to
A relationship going on twenty-six years together.
With each moment that passes, our feelings for one
Another continue to get stronger and grow more
Deeply with the passing of each day, week, month
And year. This leaves us as two of the luckiest
People that I can think of to have found one another.

When I was Young

Once in a while when I was young
I dreamed I could reach out and touch the sun,
I lay on a blanket enjoying the days
I so enjoyed just soaking up the rays,
All around me grew some deep green grass
I sat and watched as the hours pass,
On my skin that went from pale to brown
I watched as the insects moved all around,
I thought of their families so tiny and small
I looked to them so mighty and tall,
They all deserved a chance to thrive
I couldn't destroy their little lives,
As I watched them move I saw a butterfly
I watched it fly past me up into the sky,
She flew past me on delicate wings
I felt the urge to become a little thing,
I would stare at them through tiny eyes
I'd be a moth that moves and flies,
I would fly in both the day and night
I'd fly up into the bright sunlight,
I would fly around as the wind would blow
I'd fly and I would help the plants to grow,
I would nap in the flowers and sleep in the sun
I'd fly all fly all day and just have fun.

When I'm Down

Here I sit in a cold dark room,
Feeling down and full of gloom.
I'm not happy, I'm quite sad,
Reminiscing on the life I've had.
I'm feeling so down and feeling blue,
I'm not sure just what to do…
Looking out the window I see the rain,
I see the drops on my window pane.
I'd step outside, but it's too cold,
This weather makes me feel so old.
I look up to see the sky so gray,
I wish the rain would just go away.
It's been days since I've seen the sun,
Spending Tyme in the rain is never fun.
Whether you're a person or just a critter,
Bad weather sure can make you bitter.

When You're Down

SomeTymes life can bring you down,
When your happiness can't be found.
It can be hard to get through the day,
When your heart feels far away.
If you don't want to feel so bad,
And you're tired of feeling sad,
And you can't stand the way you feel
Everything can feel surreal.
It can make you start to cry,
Though you don't know the reason why,
And if you wait but no one's there,
No one can be found anywhere,
The next thing that you do is go outside
And embrace the space so open wide.
You need to relax and feel the sun,
With the warmth it gives to everyone.
You breathe deep and smell the air,
And see life flourish everywhere.
To this big world you are a part,
When you feel Love growing in your heart
In this world we all must thrive,
It's just so great to be alive.

When You're Not Here

I listen to music
When you're not here
But nothing feels real
When you're not near.
I can talk on the phone
Or watch some T.V.
Still I'm alone
When you're not with me.
I can go for a walk
I can sit in the sun
But when you're not around
Nothing seems like fun.
I spend Tyme in the garden
Just picking some flowers
But Tyme without you
Seems to go on for hours.
So come back soon
And make me feel better
Because I always feel good
When we are together.

Windows and Walls

She sits there lonely
In her trusty old chair
Reminded by memories
When life seemed more fair.
She was once young
But now her youth is gone
All that she has
Are here memories here alone.
She relives her days
That are gone out of touch
Along with the memories
She misses so much.
She thinks back when
She was much younger
And all of the family
She had here among her.
So she sits here and rocks
As she slowly recalls
The Tymes she had here
Beyond these windows and walls

With You

Let me hold you in my arms,
Let me Love you with my charms.
Please give me a little kiss,
Because it fills my heart with bliss.
Come and sit right next to me,
Because it's where I want to be.
When you're here with me tonight,
It makes everything all right.
Please come and take me by my hand
It's sure to make me feel so grand.
When you whisper in my ear,
Its all the things that I want to hear.
Please call me on the telephone,
Because I don't want to be alone.
Let me lay it on the line,
Your Love makes me feel divine.
So let me spend my life with you,
It is all I ever want to do.

Without a Trace

You lift me up when I feel sad
You make me feel good when I feel bad,
You put a smile upon my face
My sadness gone without a trace,
SomeTymes I'm left feeling small
When I do you leave me so tall,
You make me happy despite the weather
I Love when we get some Tyme together,
Of all my friends you are the best
I Love you way beyond the rest,
When I feel low you are my muse
You hold me up beyond my blues,
You are wise beyond your years
You wipe away all of my tears,
If I'm sad you hold me tight
I like to hold you all through the night,
You make things all right, when all is wrong
You always make me feel like I belong.

When I'm Alone

I'm here all alone
So I put some records on
The sounds fill the room
Still depression lingers on.
So I try the radio
But the songs that I hear
Are the ones that we heard
When you still were here.
I long for your touch
To make me feel better
I'm feeling all alone
I spite of good weather.
So please come back soon
So we can be together.
I'm feeling afraid
Nothing makes me feel good
I hope you'll be here soon
So I feel like I should.

You and I

You help make my dreams come true,
You bring me up when I feel blue.
I wish that I could do the same,
I wish didn't feel so lame.
You're so handsome and so sweet,
You make every day a treat.
I Love you for so many reasons,
I Love you in all the seasons.
You're so friendly, you're so nice,
You help fill my world with spice.
I miss you when you're not here
I Love the way you squelch my fears.
You're so helpful and so kind,
You help fix my broken mind.
I look forward to our Tyme together,
I Love spending Tyme with you, despite the weather.
You help make me feel so strong.
Your heart is where my soul belongs.
I like it when you hold my hand,
I Love the way you make me feel so grand.
You lift my spirits way up high
You give me wings so I can fly.
I Love holding you in my arms,
I Love all your stately charms.
You hold me tight when I feel down,
You are the nicest guy in town.
I just want to be your closest friend
I know we'll be together until the end.

You Are My Friend

I'm feeling so blue
I'm feeling so down
I'm always sad
When you're not around

I feel so empty
I feel so depressed
When you're not here
My life is a mess.

When I'm all alone
It's you that I miss
You could make things better
With one little kiss.

When you are here
I feel much better
I always enjoy
Our Tyme together.

I really like
Just holding your hand
And when you do
It makes me feel grand.

When you are here
I feel young again
I am so very glad
You are my friend.

You Help Me in So Many Ways

You help me when I'm feeling low,
Because of all the Love that you show.
You help me make my dreams come true,
Because of each and everything that you do.
You help me soar way up to the sky,
Because you're such a wonderful guy.
You help me to ease my mind,
Because you are always so nice and kind.
You help make me a better friend,
Because of all the Love you send.
You help me to Love so much more,
Because your heart is an open door.
You help me to give all that I can,
Because you're such a thoughtful man.
You help me to always be my best,
Because you're better than all of the rest.
You help me to reach my goal
Because you're such a giving soul.
You help me to always make my day,
Because you're giving in every way.
You help me to forever stay sane,
Because of the way you always ease my pain.
You help me to always, always care,
Because you're always, always there.

You Make Me Feel...

You make me feel like I'm the king of the world.
You make me feel like anything is possible.
You make me feel handsome like you.
You make me feel Loved the way I Love you.
You make me feel like I could dance forever.
You make me feel tall and strong.
You make me feel warm and comfy.
You make me feel lucky you're in my life.
You make me feel soft and cuddly.
You make me feel rich in emotion.
You make me feel like no one can stop me.
You make me feel thankful for your friendship.
You make me feel like I'm in heaven.
You make me feel like I must be dreaming.
You make me feel like I'm cared for.
You make me feel appreciated.
You make me feel like I'm floating on air.
You make me feel fantastic.
You make me feel accepted.
You make me feel ALIVE!

Young

When I look back to when I was young
I was supposed to be having fun.
But that was never my case,
I was just a boy erased.
How I lived in so much fear,
I wanted my mother near.
I was afraid of the boys at school,
They made me feel like a fool.
The boys, they always played so tough
I didn't want to be so rough.
I always played with all the girls,
I lived in a different world.
The girls were always nice to me,
They helped me to feel so free.
This was o.k. till I got older,
I always cried upon their shoulder.
I played with a gentle touch,
The girls, they taught me oh, so much.
I just wanted to fit in,
I was too small and way too thin.
When you are just a social outcast,
You learn how to grow up fast.

Your Love

Your Love is as solid as any stone,
With you I'll never be alone.
When I need you, I need only call,
Your Love lifts me up so tall.
You lift me up when I am weak,
Your Love is the only one I seek.
You make me strong when I feel low,
You help me make my heart to glow.
You help turn what's wrong to right,
I long to hold you through the night.
When you're not around it's you I miss,
Your Love puts me in a state of bliss.
I enjoy just holding onto your hand,
A hug from you makes me feel grand.
I'm so glad that you're my friend,
I will Love you till the very end.
When I'm with you my heart will race,
It starts with a smile right from your face.
My Love for you lingers on and on,
I'll Love you till all Tyme is gone.

Your Own Little Stars

You can see the dew
Out on the lawn,
It forms little drops
As night turns to dawn.
The wind is blowing
Through the trees,
While you sit outside
You can feel the breeze.
The birds are busy
Singing their song,
The weather's so nice
You'll want to sing along.
The sky is blue
The clouds are white,
The moon comes out
As day turns to night.
As the night sky shines
Catch lightning bugs in jars,
It's just like having
Your own little stars.

You're My Best Friend

I Love you because you're my best friend
I know we'll be together until the end,
Being by your side makes me feel proud
It makes me want to shout out loud,
When I'm by your side I feel so grand
It makes me want to hold your hand,
When the day is over I want to hold you tight
I'll hold you strong with all my might,
When I can, I enjoy a hug from you
It lifts me up when I feel blue,
When we're together I like looking at your face
It makes me feel lost in Tyme and space,
When we're alone I feel calm for a while
You make me want to share a smile,
Being with you is like I'm feeling I'm at home
You cheer me up when I'm alone,
When we're together Love starts with a kiss
Soon afterwards I'm filled with bliss,
Tyme spent with you is Tyme spent together
I know in my heart it will be forever.

You're the One I Love

You're the one that I Love
You're an angel sent from above,
You're always so kind
Your touch is so divine,
I Love holding you all night
You make what's wrong into what's right,
Just the touch of your hand
Makes me feel oh, so grand,
You can turn my day around
When I'm feeling so down,
When you give me a kiss
It fills me with bliss,
No, there's nothing better
Than spending Tyme together
I Love you because you're my best friend
We'll be together till the end.